Now I Know

Seeds

by MELVIN AND GILDA BERGER

SCHOLASTIC INC.
New York Toronto London Auckland Sydney
Mexico City New Delhi Hong Kong Buenos Aires

Cover: PA0207359; © BIOS / Peter Arnold, Inc.; page 3: © Joerg Boethling / Peter Arnold, Inc.; page 4: © Ed Reschke / Peter Arnold, Inc.; page 5: © Robert J. Erwin / Photo Researchers, Inc.; page 6: © J. Douillet / Peter Arnold, Inc.; page 7A: © Masino / Peter Arnold, Inc.; page 7B: © Byron Jorjorian / Peter Arnold, Inc.; page 8A: © Lionel Atwill / Peter Arnold, Inc.; Page 8B: © Phil A. Harrington / Peter Arnold, Inc.; page 9: © Elisa Leonelli / BRUCE COLEMAN INC.; page 10: © JORGEN SCHYTTE / Peter Arnold, Inc.; page 11: © Joerg Boethling / Peter Arnold, Inc.; page 12: © Rex Butcher / BRUCE COLEMAN INC.; page 13: © Werner H. Muller / Peter Arnold, Inc.; page 14: © Carl R. Sams II / Peter Arnold, Inc.; page 15: © Manfred Danegger / Peter Arnold, Inc.; page 16: © William Harlow / Photo Researchers, Inc.; page 17: © John Kaprielian / Photo Researchers, Inc; page 18: © Sandra Ivany / Picture Quest; page 19: © Jock Montgomery / BRUCE COLEMAN INC.; page 20: © S.J. Krasemann / Peter Arnold, Inc.; page 21: © S.J. Krasemann / Peter Arnold, Inc.; page 22: © Ernest A. Janes/ BRUCE COLEMAN INC.; page 23: © Javier Larrea/ Age fotostock; page 24: © John Hyde/ BRUCE COLEMAN INC; page 25: © Ed Reschke / Peter Arnold, Inc.; page 26: © David Cavagnaro / Peter Arnold, Inc.; page 26: © Helmut Gritscher / Peter Arnold, Inc.; page 27A: © Gilbert S. Grant / Photo Researchers, Inc.; page 27B: © Gilbert S. Grant / Photo Researchers, Inc.; page 28A: © Walter H. Hodge / Peter Arnold, Inc.; page 28B: © Kunst & Scheidulin/ AGE fotostock; page 29A: © Bios / Peter Arnold, Inc.; page 29B: © Mark E. Gibson / Corbis; page 30: © Ron Giling / Peter Arnold, Inc.; page 31 A: © Shehzad Noorani / Peter Arnold, Inc.; page 31 B: © Nick North / Corbis; page 31 B: © Royalty-Free / Corbis ; page 31 C: © Royalty-Free / Corbis; Index: © Adrianna Williams / Zefa / Corbis

ISBN-13: 978-0-439-92391-0
ISBN-10: 0-439-92391-3

22 21 20 19 18 17 16 15 14 13 12 16 17 18 19/0

Printed in the U.S.A.
First Printing, March 2007

Seeds, seeds, seeds.
There are all kinds of seeds.

An acorn is a seed.

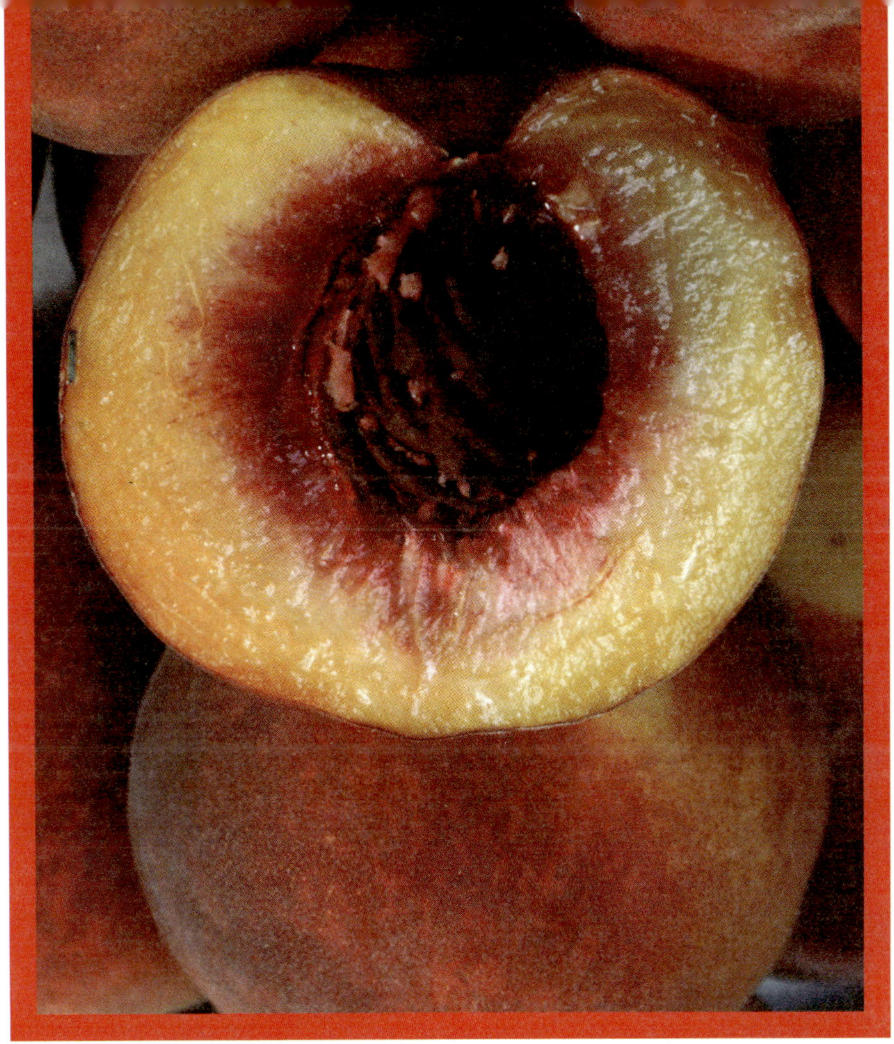

A peach pit is a seed.

Peas are seeds.

So is corn.

Strawberry seeds are tiny.

DID YOU KNOW?

The biggest coconuts weigh as much as you do!

A coconut is a giant seed.

What do seeds do?

They grow into plants.

Some seeds start to grow when they fall to the ground...

. . . or blow to other places.

Some seeds start to grow when squirrels bury them...

...or birds drop them.

Some seeds shoot out and land on the ground.

DID YOU KNOW?

Some coconuts float more than 1,000 miles!

Some seeds float onto land.

Seeds start to grow in soil.

Anyone can plant seeds.

Seeds grow down.

And seeds grow up.
It's a plant!

Plants need warmth and water to grow.

DID YOU KNOW?

Plants make the food they need from water and sunlight.

Plants also need sunlight.

Plants grow bigger and stronger.

DID YOU KNOW?

Seeds grow into plants that look like the plants they came from.

After a while they make their own seeds.

Pumpkins grow from pumpkin seeds.

Peanuts grow from peanut seeds.

Maple trees grow from
maple seeds.

Apple trees grow from apple seeds.

We all eat plants or parts of plants...

...and lots of

seeds, seeds, seeds!

GLOSSARY

Acorn: The seed of an oak tree.

Grow: To increase in size or length.

Leaves: The flat parts of plants that grow out from stems.

Pit: The large, hard seed in the middle of some fruits, such as peaches, plums, and cherries.

Plant: A living thing that makes food from air, sunlight, and water.

Root: The part of a plant that grows under the ground.

Seed: The part of a plant from which a new plant can grow.

Soil: Dirt or earth for growing plants in woods, gardens, lawns, or flower pots.

Stem: The long main part of a plant from which the leaves and flowers grow.

Sunlight: The light of the sun.